50 Back to Basics: Simple and Tasty Recipes

By: Kelly Johnson

Table of Contents

- Classic Scrambled Eggs
- Homemade Pancakes
- Simple Roasted Vegetables
- Grilled Cheese Sandwich
- Easy Chicken Stir-Fry
- Basic Spaghetti with Marinara
- Crispy Baked Potatoes
- Classic Caesar Salad
- One-Pot Beef Stew
- Quick Chicken Soup
- Simple Veggie Omelette
- Easy Beef Tacos
- Homemade Tomato Soup
- Roasted Chicken with Herbs
- Basic Mashed Potatoes
- Simple Stir-Fried Rice
- Veggie Frittata
- Spaghetti Carbonara
- Simple Baked Salmon
- Classic Meatloaf
- Garlic Butter Shrimp
- Quick Fried Rice
- Grilled Chicken Breast
- Simple Caprese Salad
- Crispy Roasted Chickpeas
- Basic Veggie Soup
- Easy Tuna Salad
- Simple Beef Chili
- Homemade Chicken Nuggets
- Quick Pesto Pasta
- Simple Cucumber Salad
- Basic Pancakes with Maple Syrup
- Easy Grilled Veggie Skewers
- Simple Chicken Parmesan
- Quick Veggie Wraps

- Fresh Guacamole with Chips
- Classic French Toast
- Simple Roasted Salmon
- Spaghetti Aglio e Olio
- Basic Veggie Burger
- Grilled Portobello Mushrooms
- Simple Egg Salad Sandwich
- Basic Fruit Salad
- Quick Chicken Tacos
- Easy Garlic Bread
- Simple Potato Salad
- Roasted Brussels Sprouts
- Classic BLT Sandwich
- Easy Baked Ziti
- Simple Chocolate Chip Cookies

Classic Scrambled Eggs

Ingredients

- 4 eggs
- 2 tbsp butter
- Salt and pepper to taste
- 1 tbsp milk (optional)

Instructions

1. Crack the eggs into a bowl and whisk with a fork until well combined. Add a pinch of salt and pepper.
2. Heat butter in a skillet over medium-low heat.
3. Pour in the eggs and let them cook undisturbed for about 30 seconds.
4. Stir gently with a spatula, pushing the eggs from the edges towards the center.
5. Continue cooking, stirring occasionally, until the eggs are just set but still slightly soft.
6. Serve immediately with toast or as desired.

Homemade Pancakes

Ingredients

- 1 cup all-purpose flour
- 2 tbsp sugar
- 1 tbsp baking powder
- 1/2 tsp salt
- 1 cup milk
- 1 egg
- 2 tbsp melted butter
- 1 tsp vanilla extract

Instructions

1. In a large bowl, whisk together the flour, sugar, baking powder, and salt.
2. In another bowl, mix the milk, egg, melted butter, and vanilla extract.
3. Pour the wet ingredients into the dry ingredients and stir until just combined (don't overmix).
4. Heat a non-stick skillet or griddle over medium heat. Lightly grease with butter or cooking spray.
5. Pour 1/4 cup of batter onto the skillet for each pancake. Cook until bubbles form on the surface, then flip and cook for another 1-2 minutes.
6. Serve with syrup, butter, and your favorite toppings.

Simple Roasted Vegetables

Ingredients

- 2 cups mixed vegetables (carrots, bell peppers, zucchini, broccoli, etc.)
- 2 tbsp olive oil
- 1 tsp garlic powder
- 1 tsp dried thyme
- Salt and pepper to taste

Instructions

1. Preheat the oven to 425°F (220°C).
2. Cut the vegetables into evenly sized pieces.
3. Toss the vegetables with olive oil, garlic powder, dried thyme, salt, and pepper.
4. Spread the vegetables in a single layer on a baking sheet.
5. Roast for 20-25 minutes, or until tender and lightly browned, stirring halfway through.
6. Serve warm as a side dish.

Grilled Cheese Sandwich

Ingredients

- 2 slices of bread
- 2 tbsp butter
- 2 slices cheddar cheese

Instructions

1. Butter one side of each slice of bread.
2. Place one slice of bread, butter side down, on a skillet over medium heat.
3. Top with the cheese slices and the second slice of bread, butter side up.
4. Grill until golden brown on both sides, about 3-4 minutes per side.
5. Serve immediately with tomato soup or your favorite side.

Easy Chicken Stir-Fry

Ingredients

- 1 lb chicken breast, thinly sliced
- 2 tbsp soy sauce
- 1 tbsp hoisin sauce (optional)
- 1 tbsp cornstarch
- 1 tbsp olive oil
- 1 cup mixed vegetables (bell peppers, carrots, broccoli, etc.)
- 2 cloves garlic, minced
- 1 tsp ginger, minced

Instructions

1. In a bowl, mix the soy sauce, hoisin sauce (if using), cornstarch, and a splash of water. Toss the chicken in the sauce mixture and set aside.
2. Heat the olive oil in a large skillet or wok over medium-high heat.
3. Add the chicken and stir-fry for 5-7 minutes, until fully cooked and lightly browned.
4. Remove the chicken and set it aside. In the same skillet, add the garlic, ginger, and mixed vegetables. Stir-fry for 3-4 minutes until tender-crisp.
5. Add the chicken back to the skillet and stir to combine. Serve over rice or noodles.

Basic Spaghetti with Marinara

Ingredients

- 8 oz spaghetti
- 1 jar (24 oz) marinara sauce
- 2 tbsp olive oil
- 2 cloves garlic, minced
- Fresh basil for garnish (optional)

Instructions

1. Cook the spaghetti according to package directions. Drain and set aside.
2. In a pan, heat olive oil over medium heat. Add garlic and cook for 1-2 minutes, until fragrant.
3. Pour in the marinara sauce and simmer for 5-7 minutes.
4. Toss the cooked spaghetti in the sauce until evenly coated.
5. Serve with fresh basil and grated parmesan if desired.

Crispy Baked Potatoes

Ingredients

- 4 medium potatoes
- 2 tbsp olive oil
- 1 tsp garlic powder
- 1 tsp paprika
- Salt and pepper to taste

Instructions

1. Preheat the oven to 400°F (200°C).
2. Wash the potatoes and pat them dry. Cut them into wedges or leave them whole.
3. Toss the potatoes with olive oil, garlic powder, paprika, salt, and pepper.
4. Spread the potatoes in a single layer on a baking sheet.
5. Bake for 30-40 minutes, flipping halfway through, until crispy and golden brown.
6. Serve with ketchup or your favorite dipping sauce.

Classic Caesar Salad

Ingredients

- 4 cups Romaine lettuce, chopped
- 1/2 cup Caesar dressing
- 1/4 cup grated parmesan cheese
- Croutons for topping

Instructions

1. In a large bowl, toss the Romaine lettuce with Caesar dressing.
2. Add the grated parmesan and toss again.
3. Top with croutons and extra parmesan.
4. Serve immediately as a side or light meal.

One-Pot Beef Stew

Ingredients

- 1 lb beef stew meat, cubed
- 4 cups beef broth
- 4 potatoes, peeled and diced
- 2 carrots, sliced
- 1 onion, chopped
- 2 cloves garlic, minced
- 1 tsp dried thyme
- Salt and pepper to taste

Instructions

1. In a large pot, brown the beef stew meat over medium heat until fully cooked, about 5-7 minutes.
2. Add the onion and garlic and sauté for 2 minutes until fragrant.
3. Pour in the beef broth and add the potatoes, carrots, thyme, salt, and pepper.
4. Bring to a boil, then reduce heat and simmer for 45 minutes to 1 hour, until the beef and vegetables are tender.
5. Serve hot and enjoy.

Quick Chicken Soup

Ingredients

- 1 lb boneless, skinless chicken breast or thighs
- 6 cups chicken broth
- 2 carrots, diced
- 2 celery stalks, diced
- 1 onion, chopped
- 2 cloves garlic, minced
- 1 tsp dried thyme
- Salt and pepper to taste
- 1 cup egg noodles or rice (optional)

Instructions

1. In a large pot, combine chicken, broth, carrots, celery, onion, garlic, thyme, salt, and pepper.
2. Bring to a boil, then reduce heat and simmer for 20-25 minutes, or until the chicken is cooked through.
3. Remove the chicken, shred it, and return it to the pot.
4. If using, add the egg noodles or rice and cook according to package instructions.
5. Serve hot, garnished with fresh herbs if desired.

Simple Veggie Omelette

Ingredients

- 2 eggs
- 1/4 cup bell peppers, diced
- 1/4 cup onions, diced
- 1/4 cup spinach, chopped
- Salt and pepper to taste
- 1 tbsp butter or oil
- Optional: cheese, mushrooms, tomatoes, or herbs

Instructions

1. Beat the eggs in a bowl and season with salt and pepper.
2. Heat butter or oil in a skillet over medium heat.
3. Add the diced vegetables and sauté for 2-3 minutes until soft.
4. Pour the beaten eggs over the vegetables, tilting the pan to ensure even coverage.
5. Cook for 2-3 minutes, then fold the omelette in half and serve.

Easy Beef Tacos

Ingredients

- 1 lb ground beef
- 1 packet taco seasoning (or homemade)
- 1/2 cup water
- 8 small taco shells or tortillas
- Toppings: lettuce, tomatoes, cheese, sour cream, salsa, etc.

Instructions

1. Brown the ground beef in a skillet over medium heat, breaking it apart as it cooks.
2. Drain excess fat, then stir in taco seasoning and water.
3. Simmer for 5-7 minutes until the sauce thickens.
4. Warm the taco shells according to package instructions.
5. Fill the shells with the beef mixture and your favorite toppings. Serve immediately.

Homemade Tomato Soup

Ingredients

- 1 can (28 oz) crushed tomatoes
- 2 cups chicken or vegetable broth
- 1 small onion, chopped
- 2 cloves garlic, minced
- 1 tsp dried basil
- 1/2 tsp sugar (optional)
- Salt and pepper to taste
- 1/4 cup heavy cream (optional)

Instructions

1. In a large pot, sauté the onion and garlic in a little oil until soft, about 3-4 minutes.
2. Add the crushed tomatoes, broth, basil, sugar, salt, and pepper.
3. Bring to a boil, then reduce heat and simmer for 15-20 minutes.
4. Use an immersion blender to purée the soup until smooth, or transfer to a blender.
5. Stir in heavy cream if desired and serve warm.

Roasted Chicken with Herbs

Ingredients

- 1 whole chicken (about 3-4 lbs)
- 2 tbsp olive oil
- 1 lemon, quartered
- 4 cloves garlic, smashed
- 1 tbsp dried rosemary
- 1 tbsp dried thyme
- Salt and pepper to taste

Instructions

1. Preheat the oven to 425°F (220°C).
2. Pat the chicken dry and rub it with olive oil, rosemary, thyme, salt, and pepper.
3. Stuff the cavity with lemon wedges and garlic.
4. Place the chicken on a roasting rack in a roasting pan.
5. Roast for 1-1.5 hours, or until the internal temperature reaches 165°F (75°C) and the skin is golden brown.
6. Let the chicken rest for 10 minutes before carving.

Basic Mashed Potatoes

Ingredients

- 2 lbs potatoes, peeled and cubed
- 1/2 cup milk
- 1/4 cup butter
- Salt and pepper to taste
- Optional: garlic, cheese, or herbs

Instructions

1. Boil the potatoes in salted water until tender, about 15-20 minutes.
2. Drain the potatoes and return them to the pot.
3. Mash with a potato masher or use a hand mixer for smoother potatoes.
4. Add butter, milk, salt, and pepper, and mix until creamy.
5. Serve warm, with optional garlic, cheese, or herbs.

Simple Stir-Fried Rice

Ingredients

- 2 cups cooked rice (preferably day-old)
- 2 tbsp soy sauce
- 1 tbsp sesame oil
- 2 eggs, lightly beaten
- 1/2 cup peas and carrots (frozen or fresh)
- 2 cloves garlic, minced
- Green onions for garnish

Instructions

1. Heat sesame oil in a skillet or wok over medium-high heat.
2. Add garlic, peas, and carrots, and stir-fry for 2-3 minutes.
3. Push the veggies to the side, and scramble the eggs in the same pan.
4. Add the cooked rice and soy sauce. Stir everything together and cook for another 3-4 minutes.
5. Garnish with green onions and serve.

Veggie Frittata

Ingredients

- 6 eggs
- 1/2 cup milk
- 1 cup mixed vegetables (spinach, peppers, onions, mushrooms)
- Salt and pepper to taste
- 1 tbsp olive oil
- 1/4 cup shredded cheese (optional)

Instructions

1. Preheat the oven to 375°F (190°C).
2. Heat olive oil in an oven-safe skillet over medium heat.
3. Sauté the vegetables until tender, about 5-7 minutes.
4. In a bowl, whisk together the eggs, milk, salt, and pepper.
5. Pour the egg mixture over the veggies and cook for 2-3 minutes, then transfer to the oven.
6. Bake for 10-15 minutes until the frittata is set.
7. Serve warm, topped with cheese if desired.

Spaghetti Carbonara

Ingredients

- 8 oz spaghetti
- 2 eggs
- 1/2 cup grated Parmesan cheese
- 4 oz pancetta or bacon, chopped
- 2 cloves garlic, minced
- Salt and pepper to taste
- Fresh parsley for garnish (optional)

Instructions

1. Cook the spaghetti according to package directions. Reserve 1 cup of pasta water, then drain.
2. In a skillet, cook pancetta or bacon over medium heat until crispy, about 5 minutes.
3. Add garlic and sauté for 1 minute.
4. In a bowl, whisk together the eggs, cheese, salt, and pepper.
5. Toss the pasta with the pancetta and garlic, then stir in the egg mixture.
6. Gradually add pasta water to achieve a creamy consistency.
7. Serve with fresh parsley.

Simple Baked Salmon

Ingredients

- 4 salmon fillets
- 2 tbsp olive oil
- 1 lemon, sliced
- Salt and pepper to taste
- Fresh herbs (dill or parsley)

Instructions

1. Preheat the oven to 400°F (200°C).
2. Place the salmon fillets on a baking sheet lined with parchment paper.
3. Drizzle with olive oil and season with salt and pepper.
4. Top each fillet with lemon slices and fresh herbs.
5. Bake for 12-15 minutes, or until the salmon flakes easily with a fork.
6. Serve with your favorite side dishes.

Classic Meatloaf

Ingredients

- 1 lb ground beef
- 1/2 cup breadcrumbs
- 1/4 cup milk
- 1 small onion, finely chopped
- 1 egg
- 1 tsp garlic powder
- 1 tsp dried oregano
- Salt and pepper to taste
- 1/2 cup ketchup
- 1 tbsp brown sugar

Instructions

1. Preheat the oven to 350°F (175°C).
2. In a large bowl, combine the ground beef, breadcrumbs, milk, onion, egg, garlic powder, oregano, salt, and pepper. Mix until well combined.
3. Shape the meat mixture into a loaf and place it in a greased baking dish.
4. In a small bowl, mix the ketchup and brown sugar. Spread the mixture over the meatloaf.
5. Bake for 1 hour, or until the internal temperature reaches 160°F (71°C).
6. Let it rest for 10 minutes before slicing and serving.

Garlic Butter Shrimp

Ingredients

- 1 lb large shrimp, peeled and deveined
- 4 tbsp butter
- 4 cloves garlic, minced
- 1/4 tsp red pepper flakes (optional)
- Salt and pepper to taste
- 1 tbsp fresh parsley, chopped
- 1 tbsp lemon juice

Instructions

1. In a large skillet, melt the butter over medium heat.
2. Add the garlic and red pepper flakes (if using), and cook for 1-2 minutes until fragrant.
3. Add the shrimp to the pan and season with salt and pepper.
4. Cook for 2-3 minutes on each side until the shrimp are pink and opaque.
5. Stir in the lemon juice and chopped parsley.
6. Serve immediately with rice or pasta.

Quick Fried Rice

Ingredients

- 2 cups cooked rice (preferably day-old)
- 2 tbsp soy sauce
- 1 tbsp sesame oil
- 1/2 cup peas and carrots (frozen or fresh)
- 2 eggs, lightly beaten
- 2 cloves garlic, minced
- 1/4 cup green onions, sliced

Instructions

1. Heat sesame oil in a large skillet or wok over medium-high heat.
2. Add garlic and sauté for 1 minute until fragrant.
3. Add the peas and carrots and cook for 3-4 minutes until softened.
4. Push the veggies to one side and scramble the eggs on the other side of the pan.
5. Add the rice and soy sauce, stirring everything together.
6. Cook for another 3-4 minutes, allowing the rice to crisp slightly.
7. Garnish with green onions and serve.

Grilled Chicken Breast

Ingredients

- 4 boneless, skinless chicken breasts
- 2 tbsp olive oil
- 1 tsp garlic powder
- 1 tsp dried oregano
- Salt and pepper to taste
- 1 lemon, sliced

Instructions

1. Preheat the grill to medium-high heat.
2. Rub the chicken breasts with olive oil and season with garlic powder, oregano, salt, and pepper.
3. Place the chicken on the grill and cook for 6-7 minutes per side, or until the internal temperature reaches 165°F (75°C).
4. During the last few minutes, add lemon slices to the grill.
5. Let the chicken rest for 5 minutes before slicing and serving.

Simple Caprese Salad

Ingredients

- 2 large tomatoes, sliced
- 8 oz fresh mozzarella, sliced
- 1/4 cup fresh basil leaves
- 2 tbsp olive oil
- 1 tbsp balsamic vinegar
- Salt and pepper to taste

Instructions

1. Arrange the tomato and mozzarella slices alternately on a platter.
2. Tuck fresh basil leaves between the slices.
3. Drizzle olive oil and balsamic vinegar over the salad.
4. Season with salt and pepper.
5. Serve immediately as a refreshing appetizer or side dish.

Crispy Roasted Chickpeas

Ingredients

- 1 can (15 oz) chickpeas, drained and rinsed
- 1 tbsp olive oil
- 1 tsp paprika
- 1/2 tsp garlic powder
- Salt and pepper to taste

Instructions

1. Preheat the oven to 400°F (200°C).
2. Pat the chickpeas dry with a towel.
3. Toss the chickpeas with olive oil, paprika, garlic powder, salt, and pepper.
4. Spread the chickpeas in a single layer on a baking sheet.
5. Roast for 25-30 minutes, shaking the pan halfway through, until the chickpeas are crispy.
6. Let cool before serving as a snack or topping for salads.

Basic Veggie Soup

Ingredients

- 2 tbsp olive oil
- 1 onion, chopped
- 2 carrots, diced
- 2 celery stalks, diced
- 3 cloves garlic, minced
- 4 cups vegetable broth
- 1 can (15 oz) diced tomatoes
- 1 tsp dried thyme
- Salt and pepper to taste
- 2 cups spinach or kale (optional)

Instructions

1. Heat olive oil in a large pot over medium heat.
2. Add onion, carrots, celery, and garlic. Cook for 5-7 minutes, until softened.
3. Add the vegetable broth, diced tomatoes, thyme, salt, and pepper.
4. Bring to a boil, then reduce to a simmer and cook for 20-25 minutes.
5. Stir in spinach or kale, if using, and cook for another 5 minutes.
6. Serve warm.

Easy Tuna Salad

Ingredients

- 1 can (5 oz) tuna, drained
- 1/4 cup mayonnaise
- 1 tbsp Dijon mustard
- 1 tbsp lemon juice
- Salt and pepper to taste
- 1/4 cup celery, diced
- 1/4 cup red onion, diced

Instructions

1. In a bowl, combine tuna, mayonnaise, Dijon mustard, and lemon juice.
2. Stir in celery and red onion.
3. Season with salt and pepper to taste.
4. Serve on a bed of greens, in a sandwich, or with crackers.

Simple Beef Chili

Ingredients

- 1 lb ground beef
- 1 onion, chopped
- 2 cloves garlic, minced
- 1 can (15 oz) kidney beans, drained and rinsed
- 1 can (15 oz) diced tomatoes
- 1 tbsp chili powder
- 1 tsp cumin
- Salt and pepper to taste

Instructions

1. In a large pot, brown the ground beef over medium heat.
2. Add the onion and garlic, cooking until softened.
3. Stir in the beans, diced tomatoes, chili powder, cumin, salt, and pepper.
4. Simmer for 20-25 minutes, stirring occasionally.
5. Serve with sour cream, cheese, or cornbread.

Homemade Chicken Nuggets

Ingredients

- 2 boneless, skinless chicken breasts, cut into bite-sized pieces
- 1 cup breadcrumbs
- 1/2 cup grated Parmesan cheese
- 2 eggs, beaten
- 1/2 tsp garlic powder
- Salt and pepper to taste
- Vegetable oil for frying

Instructions

1. In a shallow bowl, mix breadcrumbs, Parmesan cheese, garlic powder, salt, and pepper.
2. Dip each chicken piece into the beaten eggs, then coat with the breadcrumb mixture.
3. Heat vegetable oil in a skillet over medium-high heat.
4. Fry the chicken pieces for 3-4 minutes per side, until golden brown and cooked through.
5. Drain on paper towels and serve with dipping sauce.

Quick Pesto Pasta

Ingredients

- 8 oz pasta of choice
- 1/2 cup pesto sauce
- 1 tbsp olive oil
- 1/4 cup grated Parmesan cheese
- Salt and pepper to taste

Instructions

1. Cook the pasta according to package directions.
2. Drain the pasta, reserving 1/2 cup of pasta water.
3. In a large bowl, toss the pasta with pesto, olive oil, and reserved pasta water to coat.
4. Season with salt and pepper to taste.
5. Sprinkle with Parmesan cheese and serve warm.

Simple Cucumber Salad

Ingredients

- 2 cucumbers, thinly sliced
- 1/4 cup red onion, thinly sliced
- 2 tbsp olive oil
- 1 tbsp white vinegar
- 1/2 tsp salt
- 1/4 tsp black pepper
- 1 tbsp fresh dill, chopped (optional)

Instructions

1. In a large bowl, combine the cucumber and red onion.
2. Drizzle with olive oil and vinegar, and toss to coat.
3. Season with salt and pepper.
4. Garnish with fresh dill, if desired.
5. Serve chilled as a refreshing side dish.

Basic Pancakes with Maple Syrup

Ingredients

- 1 cup all-purpose flour
- 2 tbsp sugar
- 1 tsp baking powder
- 1/2 tsp baking soda
- 1/4 tsp salt
- 1 cup buttermilk
- 1 large egg
- 2 tbsp melted butter
- Maple syrup for serving

Instructions

1. In a large bowl, whisk together the flour, sugar, baking powder, baking soda, and salt.
2. In another bowl, whisk the buttermilk, egg, and melted butter.
3. Pour the wet ingredients into the dry ingredients and stir until just combined (it's okay if the batter is a little lumpy).
4. Heat a nonstick skillet or griddle over medium heat and lightly grease with butter.
5. Pour about 1/4 cup of batter onto the skillet for each pancake. Cook until bubbles form on the surface, then flip and cook until golden brown on both sides.
6. Serve warm with maple syrup.

Easy Grilled Veggie Skewers

Ingredients

- 1 zucchini, sliced into rounds
- 1 bell pepper, cut into chunks
- 1 red onion, cut into chunks
- 8 oz mushrooms, whole or halved
- 2 tbsp olive oil
- 1 tbsp balsamic vinegar
- 1 tsp dried oregano
- Salt and pepper to taste

Instructions

1. Preheat the grill to medium-high heat.
2. In a bowl, toss the vegetables with olive oil, balsamic vinegar, oregano, salt, and pepper.
3. Thread the vegetables onto skewers, alternating the types.
4. Grill the skewers for 8-10 minutes, turning occasionally, until the vegetables are tender and slightly charred.
5. Serve as a side dish or with rice.

Simple Chicken Parmesan

Ingredients

- 4 boneless, skinless chicken breasts
- 1 cup breadcrumbs
- 1/2 cup grated Parmesan cheese
- 1 egg, beaten
- 1 1/2 cups marinara sauce
- 1 1/2 cups shredded mozzarella cheese
- 1 tbsp olive oil

Instructions

1. Preheat the oven to 375°F (190°C).
2. In a shallow bowl, mix breadcrumbs and Parmesan cheese. Dip the chicken breasts into the egg, then coat with the breadcrumb mixture.
3. Heat olive oil in a skillet over medium heat. Brown the chicken breasts on both sides (about 3-4 minutes per side).
4. Place the browned chicken on a baking sheet, top with marinara sauce and mozzarella cheese.
5. Bake for 20-25 minutes, or until the chicken reaches 165°F (75°C) and the cheese is melted and bubbly.
6. Serve with pasta or a side salad.

Quick Veggie Wraps

Ingredients

- 1 cup hummus
- 1 large whole wheat tortilla
- 1/2 cup shredded carrots
- 1/2 cucumber, thinly sliced
- 1/4 cup red bell pepper, thinly sliced
- 1/4 cup spinach or lettuce

Instructions

1. Spread a generous layer of hummus over the tortilla.
2. Arrange the shredded carrots, cucumber, bell pepper, and spinach in the center.
3. Roll up the tortilla, folding in the sides as you go.
4. Slice into halves and serve as a light lunch or snack.

Fresh Guacamole with Chips

Ingredients

- 2 ripe avocados, mashed
- 1/4 cup red onion, finely chopped
- 1 small tomato, diced
- 1 tbsp lime juice
- 1/2 tsp garlic powder
- Salt and pepper to taste
- Tortilla chips for serving

Instructions

1. In a bowl, mash the avocados with a fork.
2. Stir in the onion, tomato, lime juice, garlic powder, salt, and pepper.
3. Taste and adjust seasoning if needed.
4. Serve with tortilla chips for dipping.

Classic French Toast

Ingredients

- 2 slices of bread (preferably thick-cut)
- 1 egg
- 1/4 cup milk
- 1/2 tsp vanilla extract
- 1/4 tsp cinnamon
- Butter for cooking
- Maple syrup for serving

Instructions

1. In a shallow bowl, whisk together the egg, milk, vanilla extract, and cinnamon.
2. Heat a skillet or griddle over medium heat and add a small amount of butter.
3. Dip each slice of bread into the egg mixture, ensuring both sides are coated.
4. Cook the bread on the skillet for 2-3 minutes per side, or until golden brown.
5. Serve with maple syrup.

Simple Roasted Salmon

Ingredients

- 4 salmon fillets
- 2 tbsp olive oil
- 1 lemon, sliced
- 1 tsp dried dill
- Salt and pepper to taste

Instructions

1. Preheat the oven to 400°F (200°C).
2. Place the salmon fillets on a baking sheet lined with parchment paper.
3. Drizzle olive oil over the salmon, then top with lemon slices, dill, salt, and pepper.
4. Roast for 12-15 minutes, or until the salmon easily flakes with a fork.
5. Serve with steamed vegetables or rice.

Spaghetti Aglio e Olio

Ingredients

- 8 oz spaghetti
- 4 cloves garlic, thinly sliced
- 1/4 tsp red pepper flakes
- 1/4 cup olive oil
- 1/4 cup fresh parsley, chopped
- Salt to taste
- Grated Parmesan for serving (optional)

Instructions

1. Cook the spaghetti according to package directions. Drain, reserving 1/2 cup of pasta water.
2. While the pasta cooks, heat olive oil in a large skillet over medium heat. Add garlic and red pepper flakes, cooking for 1-2 minutes until fragrant.
3. Add the cooked spaghetti to the skillet, along with the reserved pasta water. Toss to combine.
4. Stir in fresh parsley and season with salt.
5. Serve with a sprinkle of grated Parmesan if desired.

Basic Veggie Burger

Ingredients

- 1 can (15 oz) black beans, drained and mashed
- 1/2 cup breadcrumbs
- 1/4 cup grated carrot
- 1/4 cup finely chopped onion
- 1 tsp garlic powder
- 1 tbsp soy sauce
- Salt and pepper to taste
- Olive oil for frying

Instructions

1. In a bowl, combine the mashed black beans, breadcrumbs, carrot, onion, garlic powder, soy sauce, salt, and pepper.
2. Form the mixture into 4 patties.
3. Heat olive oil in a skillet over medium heat. Cook the patties for 3-4 minutes per side, until golden brown.
4. Serve on buns with your favorite toppings.

Grilled Portobello Mushrooms

Ingredients

- 4 large Portobello mushroom caps
- 2 tbsp olive oil
- 1 tbsp balsamic vinegar
- 1 tsp dried thyme
- Salt and pepper to taste

Instructions

1. Preheat the grill to medium-high heat.
2. In a small bowl, whisk together olive oil, balsamic vinegar, thyme, salt, and pepper.
3. Brush the mushroom caps with the marinade on both sides.
4. Grill the mushrooms for about 5-7 minutes per side, until tender and juicy.
5. Serve as a side dish or on a bun for a vegetarian burger.

Simple Egg Salad Sandwich

Ingredients

- 4 boiled eggs, peeled and chopped
- 2 tbsp mayonnaise
- 1 tsp Dijon mustard
- 1 tbsp chopped green onions
- Salt and pepper to taste
- 4 slices of bread

Instructions

1. In a bowl, combine the chopped eggs, mayonnaise, Dijon mustard, green onions, salt, and pepper.
2. Spread the egg salad mixture onto two slices of bread.
3. Top with the remaining bread slices to make the sandwich.
4. Serve with chips or a side salad.

Basic Fruit Salad

Ingredients

- 1 apple, diced
- 1 banana, sliced
- 1 cup strawberries, hulled and sliced
- 1/2 cup grapes, halved
- 1 orange, peeled and segmented
- 1 tbsp honey (optional)
- 1 tbsp fresh lemon juice

Instructions

1. In a large bowl, combine all the prepared fruit.
2. Drizzle with honey (optional) and fresh lemon juice.
3. Toss gently to mix.
4. Serve chilled as a refreshing snack or side dish.

Quick Chicken Tacos

Ingredients

- 2 cups cooked chicken, shredded
- 1 tbsp olive oil
- 1 packet taco seasoning
- 8 small tortillas
- 1 cup shredded lettuce
- 1/2 cup salsa
- 1/4 cup sour cream
- Shredded cheese (optional)

Instructions

1. In a skillet, heat olive oil over medium heat.
2. Add the shredded chicken and taco seasoning. Stir to coat and heat through.
3. Warm the tortillas in the microwave or on the stove.
4. Fill each tortilla with the chicken mixture, and top with lettuce, salsa, sour cream, and cheese.
5. Serve immediately.

Easy Garlic Bread

Ingredients

- 1 loaf French bread or baguette
- 4 tbsp butter, softened
- 2 cloves garlic, minced
- 1 tbsp fresh parsley, chopped
- Salt to taste

Instructions

1. Preheat the oven to 375°F (190°C).
2. Slice the bread in half lengthwise.
3. In a small bowl, mix the softened butter, garlic, parsley, and salt.
4. Spread the garlic butter mixture evenly over the cut sides of the bread.
5. Place the bread on a baking sheet and bake for 10-12 minutes until golden and crispy.
6. Slice and serve.

Simple Potato Salad

Ingredients

- 4 large potatoes, peeled and cubed
- 1/4 cup mayonnaise
- 1 tbsp Dijon mustard
- 1/4 cup chopped celery
- 1/4 cup chopped red onion
- Salt and pepper to taste

Instructions

1. Boil the potatoes in a large pot of salted water until tender, about 10-15 minutes. Drain and let cool.
2. In a large bowl, mix together mayonnaise, Dijon mustard, celery, onion, salt, and pepper.
3. Add the cooled potatoes to the dressing and toss to combine.
4. Chill in the refrigerator for at least 30 minutes before serving.

Roasted Brussels Sprouts

Ingredients

- 1 lb Brussels sprouts, trimmed and halved
- 2 tbsp olive oil
- Salt and pepper to taste
- 1 tbsp balsamic vinegar (optional)

Instructions

1. Preheat the oven to 400°F (200°C).
2. Toss the Brussels sprouts with olive oil, salt, and pepper.
3. Spread them in a single layer on a baking sheet.
4. Roast for 20-25 minutes, stirring halfway through, until crispy on the edges and tender in the middle.
5. Drizzle with balsamic vinegar, if desired, and serve hot.

Classic BLT Sandwich

Ingredients

- 4 slices of bread
- 4 slices cooked bacon
- Lettuce leaves
- 2 slices tomato
- Mayonnaise

Instructions

1. Toast the bread slices to your desired crispiness.
2. Spread mayonnaise on one side of each slice of toast.
3. Layer the bacon, lettuce, and tomato on one slice of bread.
4. Top with the second slice of bread, mayo side down.
5. Slice and serve.

Easy Baked Ziti

Ingredients

- 1 lb ziti pasta
- 2 cups marinara sauce
- 1 1/2 cups ricotta cheese
- 2 cups shredded mozzarella cheese
- 1/2 cup grated Parmesan cheese

Instructions

1. Preheat the oven to 375°F (190°C).
2. Cook the ziti pasta according to package instructions. Drain and return to the pot.
3. Stir in marinara sauce and ricotta cheese.
4. Pour the pasta mixture into a greased baking dish and top with mozzarella and Parmesan cheese.
5. Bake for 25-30 minutes, until bubbly and golden.
6. Serve with garlic bread or a salad.

Simple Chocolate Chip Cookies

Ingredients

- 1 cup unsalted butter, softened
- 3/4 cup sugar
- 3/4 cup brown sugar
- 2 tsp vanilla extract
- 2 eggs
- 2 1/4 cups all-purpose flour
- 1 tsp baking soda
- 1/2 tsp salt
- 2 cups chocolate chips

Instructions

1. Preheat the oven to 375°F (190°C).
2. In a large bowl, cream together the butter, sugar, and brown sugar.
3. Add the vanilla extract and eggs, and mix until combined.
4. In a separate bowl, combine the flour, baking soda, and salt. Gradually add to the wet ingredients.
5. Stir in the chocolate chips.
6. Drop spoonfuls of dough onto a baking sheet and bake for 9-11 minutes, until golden.
7. Cool on a wire rack and enjoy.

www.ingramcontent.com/pod-product-compliance
Lightning Source LLC
LaVergne TN
LVHW081331060526
838201LV00055B/2570